Philippians

Ben Weeks

Copyright 2016 by Ben Weeks.
The book author retains sole copyright to
his contributions to this book.
Published 2016.
Printed in the United States of America.

All rights reserved.

No portion of this book may be reproduced, stored in a retrieval system, or transmitted in any form or by any means – electronic, mechanical, photocopy, recording, scanning, or other – except for brief quotations in critical reviews or articles, without the prior written permission of the author.

ISBN 978-1-946234-02-5

Front cover design by Mark Gauthier.

This book was published by BookCrafters,
Parker, Colorado.
bookcrafterscolorado@gmail.com

This book may be ordered from
www.bookcrafters.net and other online bookstores.

Foreword

Thank you for selecting this volume of the Expository series. These volumes are the contribution of various Apostolic writers. Their biography is on the back cover. The publishers of the Expository series would like to extend a thank you for helping us get this valuable material into the hands of readers.

The desire is that people would read the scriptures and be blessed. These commentary works, or works of Expository subjects, will give insight to, and further the understanding of the readers.

Each of these authors hold the values of the original Apostles of Jesus Christ. These writers want to hold to the values expostulated in the New Testament by Jesus and his disciples. Each of them ascribe to the concept offered by the Apostle John, " I have no greater joy than to hear that my children walk in truth".

Truth has been passed down through generations and has survived critics and doubters. Truth will prevail and ultimately triumph.

These writings are our contribution to the river of written truth that has flowed down through the ages.

Read and be blessed.

Kenneth Bow

Introduction

Authorship. The letter of encouragement to Philippian believers is credited to the apostle Paul. He places his name at the beginning of the first sentence. As the founding missionary of the church, deep love and affection for the saints at Philippi are expressed throughout the short book. Paul's writing style and doctrinal emphasis are evident, especially when compared with his other epistles.

Rome has been indicated as the most likely site from which the epistle to Philippi was written. Several times, Paul refers to his "bonds" – which appears to suggest his imprisonment at Rome. Other clues within the epistle seem to concur. Although a prisoner, he was allowed some privileges. While at Rome, he was given the freedom to entertain guests (Acts 28:30). Clearly, from what is written to the Philippians, we gather that protégés such as Timothy and Epaphroditus were able to visit with Paul during his confinement and also serve as his couriers.

Philippians was probably written about 60 A.D. It was during Paul's second missionary journey, perhaps around 50 A.D., that the assembly at Philippi was originally established. The apostle wrote this fatherly treatise approximately 10 years later. Though apart for a decade or more, there had remained a devoted attachment between the apostle and the thriving congregation.

The Church. The birth of the Philippian congregation is found in Acts 16. While Paul had intended to visit Asia with the Gospel, God instead sent him to Macedonia. One of the main cities of the region was Philippi. It was considered a crucial crossroads for business in the Roman Empire. The more prominent inhabitants were known to pride themselves in their Roman citizenship. Philippi would become the location for the first church in Europe.

Customarily, when he arrived in a new area, Paul would find the Jewish synagogue and begin witnessing (Acts 14:1). However, in Philippi, it is probable that no synagogue existed, so the apostle discovered that a few women gathered on the Sabbath for a riverside prayer meeting. There he found his first convert.

Lydia, an affluent native of Thyatira, another great city of Macedonia, eagerly welcomed the message preached by Paul. Upon conversion, she opened her home to the apostles. From this inauspicious beginning, a mighty church blossomed and flourished.

But progress was not without tremendous costs. Paul and Silas were soon accosted by a tormented damsel in the crowded city. Paul tolerated the harassment for several days. But finally, he demanded the spirit to abandon the young woman. In that moment, it became apparent she had been miraculously cured.

Rather than receive the news with gladness, city leaders were appalled at the transformation of the damsel. Paul and Silas were treated to public flogging and imprisonment. But the gospel preachers were not defeated in spirit. The midnight hour found them boldly praising God. Soon an earthquake shook the prison in such vigorous fashion that "immediately all the doors were opened, and every one's bands were loosed" (Acts 16:26). This experience served to provide a wider audience for the apostle's message.

The Theme. The word "joy" appears several times in this book. Throughout his various writings, Paul plainly declares that he is well acquainted with suffering. Nowhere are his troubles more candidly described than in the book of Philippians, yet he also insists that joyful endurance is possible. He writes as a prisoner awaiting trial. However, it is apparent his main concern is not his own discomfort. Instead, he exhorts church members "that he which hath begun a good work in you will perform it until the day of Jesus Christ" (Philippians 1:6).

Every word communicates that his personal outlook is cheerful. He offers guidelines for the proper Christian attitude to the believers at Philippi, directing them to fill their minds with what is "lovely" and of "good report" (Philippians 4:8).

The pattern is repeated often throughout the ministry of Paul. Incredible opposition appears to effectively halt his endeavors to deliver the word of salvation. And yet the adversary's attempts to block the gospel from reaching lost souls ultimately constructs a far larger platform for proclaiming Christ than would have otherwise been available. When this principle is understood and embraced, it delivers a reason for rejoicing.

Philippians 1

1.1 Paul and Timotheus, the servants of Jesus Christ, to all the saints in Christ Jesus which are at Philippi, with the bishops and deacons:

1.1 True unselfishness is evident in the first words of the epistle to the Philippians. The names of two gospel-bearers, Paul and Timothy, are introduced on the same footing. Elsewhere, Timothy is addressed as a son in the gospel. But here, the younger minister is included as an equal. The legendary apostle shares credit with the lesser-experienced co-laborer in the work of the Lord. The two are servants together.

The Greek term for "servant" could perhaps be more accurately rendered "slave." Whereas servants were more akin to modern employees, slaves had absolutely no rights and no lives of their own, belonging solely to their owners. The preachers of the gospel were willingly the exclusive property of their master Jesus Christ.

The addressees are called "saints." With a single word, Paul underscores their status as "separated ones." This theme is interwoven throughout the texture of scripture. God expects his people to uphold a higher standard. Sanctification is a term closely related to this idea and appears repeatedly in the letters of Paul.

This type of identity was what God had in mind for Israel as he secured their release from Egypt. He had Moses tell them, "For thou art an holy people unto the Lord thy God: the Lord thy God hath chosen thee to be a special people unto himself, above all people that are upon the face of the earth" (Deuteronomy 7:6).

1.2-5 Grace be unto you, and peace, from God our Father, and from the Lord Jesus Christ. 3 I thank my God upon every remembrance of you, 4 Always in every prayer of mine for you all making request with joy, 5 For your fellowship in the gospel from the first day until now;

1.2-1.5 An intense affection is expressed for the congregation at Philippi. Such is the attachment that Paul mentions their needs to God each time he prays. Furthermore, his love is so great for them; every memory of the Philippian believers is treasured. His time of intercession on their behalf was not freighted with a sense of burdensome obligation. Instead, his repeated petitions for them evoked tremendous joy within him.

1.6 Being confident of this very thing, that he which hath begun a good work in you will perform it until the day of Jesus Christ:

1.6 Also communicated is an unwavering confidence that God continues to work mightily in the Philippian assembly. The author waxes prophetic regarding the church at Philippi. The days of its sensational infancy were only a taste of what was yet to be. They would witness a supernatural performance of God's power in the future.

1.7-8 Even as it is meet for me to think this of you all, because I have you in my heart; inasmuch as both in my bonds, and in the defence and confirmation of the gospel, ye all are partakers of my grace. 8 For God is my record, how greatly I long after you all in the bowels of Jesus Christ.

1.7-8 The saints are commended, not only for accepting the teachings of the apostle, but for staunchly defending and confirming the gospel message. The precious knowledge imparted to them had been esteemed to such a high degree; they were willing to fight for it.

1.9 And this I pray, that your love may abound yet more and more in knowledge and in all judgment;

1.9 Although the accomplishments were many, there were areas that needed attention. As spiritual overseer, Paul mentions how Christian love should ever be on the increase, along with a cultivation of spiritual understanding, and the development of the ability to make wise decisions.

1.10-11 That ye may approve things that are excellent; that ye may be sincere and without offence till the day of Christ. 11 Being filled with the fruits of righteousness, which are by Jesus Christ, unto the glory and praise of God.

1.10-1.11 A spirit of excellence should be pursued in all things. The authentic Christian church cannot afford to place a stamp of approval on every innovative idea. Diverse schools of thought will spring up here and there. Forward thinking progressives will always be sharing new angles and perspectives. Never lose sight of the fact that everything must be viewed through the lens of the Word. Don't just accept something simply because it is the latest fad.

The Christian assembly should not resemble the curious philosophers of Mars Hill, who gathered for the purpose of hearing "some new thing" (Acts 17:21). Instead, Bible believers are encouraged "to give the more earnest heed to the things which we have heard" (Hebrews 2:1). As David refused the armor of Saul because he had not yet proven it (I Samuel 17:39), so also should the people of God exercise similar caution.

Before fresh concepts are introduced, they have to first pass the truth test. Regardless of its popularity, whatever is offered must be conducive to godliness and beneficial to the body of Christ. Lacking this criteria, it should be discarded. Anything touted to bring positive change to the collective body of believers can only be recognized and respected after a thorough testing. Anytime approval is voiced, it should follow a rigorous examination by seasoned leaders who have proven bona fides.

Followers of Jesus should be utterly lacking in hypocrisy. To be sincere is to be without pretense and without guile. The life lived in total abandonment to Christ ought to give absolutely no occasion of causing others to stumble. Righteous living brings enormous benefits, otherwise referred to as fruitfulness, which ultimately brings glory to God!

1.12 But I would ye should understand, brethren, that the things which happened unto me have fallen out rather unto the furtherance of the gospel;

1.12 Christ is a sure inoculation against overwhelming despair. Buoyant spirits despite besetting circumstances is a trademark characteristic of apostle Paul. He insists that what appeared to be misfortunes have actually bolstered him toward his God-inspired goals. What seemed like irreversible setbacks instead led to astounding progress.

In the Greek, "furtherance" actually references the clearing of a path through dense forest undergrowth. Adversity had blazed a trail, as it were, so that the gospel eventually reached its desired destination.

1.13 So that my bonds in Christ are manifest in all the palace, and in all other places;

1.13 The apostle's message had spread as high as the most prominent household of Rome, the palace of Caesar himself. Because of Paul's status as political prisoner, he was closely watched twenty-four hours a day by the Praetorian Guard, an elite group of Roman soldiers who had each been hand-picked by the Emperor. As the guards kept him company in six-hour shifts, many of them were converted and transformed by their brief encounter with the apostle.

Rather than be dismayed and silenced by his incarceration, Paul instead found new avenues for sharing the death, burial, and resurrection of Christ. Far from the intended effect of ushering him into isolation and oblivion, his bonds rather brought about a broader spectrum of ministry. Imprisonment opened exciting new doors for making disciples.

1.14 And many of the brethren in the Lord, waxing confident by my bonds, are much more bold to speak the word without fear.

1.14 Not only did persecution produce astonishing boldness in Paul, his example inspired other disciples to follow in his footsteps. Fellow Christians were emboldened and encouraged to speak out in regard to their faith. Some believers lost all fearfulness upon observing Paul's resilience while suffering under the heavy hand of the mighty Roman government.

1.15-18 Some indeed preach Christ even of envy and strife; and some also of good will: 16 The one preach Christ of contention, not sincerely, supposing to add affliction to my bonds: 17 But the other of love, knowing that I am set for the defence of the gospel. 18 What then? notwithstanding, every way, whether in pretence, or in truth, Christ is preached; and I therein do rejoice, yea, and will rejoice.

1.15-1.18 Everyone who preached did not do so out of an authentic calling. Some proclaimed Christ out of misguided motives. Some used the message of Jesus as a platform for disagreement with another philosophy of life or religious persuasion. Some took the finer points of Christianity and argued them for the sake of an interesting debate.

Paul was not of such a narrow mind that he spent all his time denouncing the ministries of others. Instead he remained focused. He kept his gaze locked onto the main goal: delivering the life-changing new-birth message. He held unwaveringly to his purpose. Later in the epistle, he will write, "This one thing I do..." (Philippians 4:13). Here is a man who refuses distraction. He shrugs at the reports coming in about the methods of unscrupulous so-called preachers. He adamantly resists being pulled into the vortex of innuendo and gossip.

When news of certain contentious personalities reaches him, the apostle chooses to view the situation cheerfully. He rejoices that Christ is the subject being discussed. Although the messengers may be tainted by base ambitions, the superlative topic any speaker could possibly select is Jesus Christ. And in that incontrovertible truth, Paul finds solace.

1.19 For I know that this shall turn to my salvation through your prayer, and the supply of the Spirit of Jesus Christ,

1.19 The founder of the church at Philippi had a great deal of confidence in the prayers of God's people. He understood, as fellow apostle James did, that "the effectual, fervent prayer of a righteous man availeth much" (James 5:16). The prayer of one saint can make a difference. How much more powerful is corporate prayer? The aging elder was convinced their faithful petitions would result in his eventual deliverance from prison. No doubt, this is what he means by the phrase "this shall turn to my salvation."

Paul also admitted his complete dependence on the Spirit of God. He recognized it (the Spirit) not as a one-time gift, but as an oft-repeated experience. Expressed here is a desire for a continual flow of anointing.

1.20 According to my earnest expectation and my hope, that in nothing I shall be ashamed, but that with all boldness, as always, so now also Christ shall be magnified in my body, whether it be by life, or by death.

1.20 The believer can rest in the hope that to continue living is to find fulfillment in the will of God. It also brings comfort to know that passing from this life will bring eternal reward. For Paul, to abandon earthly flesh and be with Christ was certainly preferred but to abide among mortals and further the gospel was beneficial to those he dearly loved.

1.21 For to me to live is Christ, and to die is gain.

1.21 Facing death courageously, the apostle was fully assured of the awaiting glories of eternity. At the same moment, he was willing to remain on earth, anticipating more opportunities to share the plan of salvation with souls who had yet to hear the truth of God's Word.

1.22 But if I live in the flesh, this is the fruit of my labour: yet what I shall choose I wot not.

1.22 Missionary endeavors had proven exceedingly fruitful for Paul. A certain fulfillment is experienced when one is unreservedly engaged in the will of God. Jesus referred to this when he told his disciples, "I have meat to eat that ye know not of" (John 4:32). He later explained to them exactly what he meant. "Jesus saith unto them, My meat is to do the will of him that sent me, and to finish his work" (John 4:34).

1.23-24 For I am in a strait betwixt two, having a desire to depart, and to be with Christ; which is far better: 24 Nevertheless to abide in the flesh is more needful for you.

1.23-24 Cognizant that the end of his ministry is in sight, a resolved peace of mind is confidently expressed by Paul. Death holds little dread. Departing mortal existence proffers no terror whatsoever. For the faithful, crossing the border between our worldly dwelling into life everlasting is eagerly anticipated. The apostle had visited paradise and had momentarily tasted a sample of the world to come (II Corinthians 12:4). Without question, the fleeting experience had created a wistful longing to traverse that great divide.

Lasting treasures were laid up to be received following death. Elsewhere, Paul had written of a "crown of righteousness" yet to be given Christians (II Timothy 4:8). He also had written, "Set your affection on things above, not on things on the earth" (Colossians 3:2).

The forward progress of believers was measured and celebrated. And yet the ultimate forward move was leaving his dutiful care as a spiritual father and going to be with Christ. This would become the climactic culmination of successful soul-winning labor.

1.25-26 And having this confidence, I know that I shall abide and continue with you all for your furtherance and joy of faith; 26 That your rejoicing

may be more abundant in Jesus Christ for me by my coming to you again.

1.25-1.26 Torn between these two forceful yet opposing inclinations, Paul relishes the obvious blessings that his ministerial investments had brought forth in the congregants. Qualities such as maturity and joyfulness are commended.

1.27 Only let your conversation be as it becometh the gospel of Christ: that whether I come and see you, or else be absent, I may hear of your affairs, that ye stand fast in one spirit, with one mind striving together for the faith of the gospel;

1.27 It should always be remembered that saints represent the gospel in their ordinary, everyday lives. Perhaps the most impressive testimony to non-Christians is the exceptional example of unity among those who believe. Psalm 133:1 urges us toward this type of oneness: "Behold, how good and how pleasant it is for brethren to dwell together in unity!"

Jesus addressed this competitive impulse in his disciples, knowing they were prone to jostle one another in their quest for personal exaltation, he said, "By this shall all men know that ye are my disciples, if ye have love one to another" (John 13:35).

1.28 And in nothing terrified by your adversaries: which is to them an evident token of perdition, but to you of salvation, and that of God.

1.28 Another outstanding feature of authentic Christianity is the way in which Christ-followers endure assault from enemies. For the apostle, the thrill of witnessing the power of the spirit transforming sinners caused the inevitable persecutions to lose every tendency to incite fear and reluctance.

Paul pushes his readers toward relinquishing all terror. This is possible when they realize their attackers, by their actions, have procured their own doom. And yet at the same time, have assured greater rewards for enduring believers.

1.29-30 For unto you it is given in the behalf of Christ, not only to believe on him, but also to suffer for his sake; 30 Having the same conflict which ye saw in me, and now hear to be in me.

1.29-1.30 Suffering should be embraced as a natural part of the Christian experience. Just as Christ willingly subjected himself to the cross, we should accept the fact that we, too, will be endure affliction on his behalf. As the accomplished missionary who gloried in his infirmities, Paul exhorts adherents toward the same perspective.

Philippians 2

2.1 If there be therefore any consolation in Christ, if any comfort of love, if any fellowship of the Spirit, if any bowels and mercies,

2.1 Paul exhorts the saints toward Christian charity. Believers should be actively encouraging and comforting one another. "If" does not denote any doubts about whether these characteristics of godly love are present. Rather, this figure of speech is used to emphasize what behaviors are expected of the Christian.

Utilized here are literary methods of expression commonly called first class conditional clauses. Coveted attributes are introduced in the assumption that believers already understand these traits are resident within the body of Christ.

Perhaps it could more easily read, "Since there is encouragement in Christ, and there definitely is..." And, "Since there is comfort, and there most certainly is…" Paul understands that the Philippian believers already know enough about Christ that many of these Christian qualities should reasonably follow conversion.

"Bowels" refers to a sincere affection that originates deeply within the innermost being. In modern terminology, this type of expression could more accurately be rendered "heart-felt depths of compassion."

2.2 Fulfil ye my joy, that ye be likeminded, having the same love, being of one accord, of one mind.

2.2 For Paul, joy would not be derived from a quick release from Roman chains. His joy was not contingent upon his exoneration from all criminal charges. The source of his joy was not the hopeful expectation of the restoration of personal comfort or a transferal to luxurious living quarters.

True joy would finally be realized upon the achievement of unity. Laboring together toward common spiritual objectives: this was the worthy aim.

Philippian congregants were not admonished to be exactly alike, but rather to be "like-minded" – keeping the spread of the gospel as their foremost priority.

The church had a foundation of wide diversity. Lydia, a seller of purple, was evidently wealthy and had contacts among the highest tiers of society. The unnamed damsel, whose deliverance is detailed in Acts 16, obviously had little control over her own life. What income she received from her extraordinary powers of divination went directly to her masters. She seemed to be nothing more than a mere slave. However, her menial social standing did not preclude her from entrance into the kingdom of God.

How beautiful to observe the work of the Spirit at every level – from the greatest of the community to the least. Furthermore, the conversion of the Philippian keeper of the prison must not be forgotten. Baptized with his entire household on the same night of the miraculous earthquake, the jailer represents neither the extremely wealthy nor the impoverished. He might be more aptly described as belonging to the laboring class. The far-reaching arm of the salvation message is capable of finding and rescuing needy souls at every strata.

2.3 Let nothing be done through strife or vainglory; but in lowliness of mind let each esteem other better than themselves.

2.3 Actions and motives should be weighed carefully. The believer should not be motivated out of vengeful thoughts and desires. Nor should he act with the intention of procuring a competitive advantage over a brother.

Jesus reprimanded his followers for their assertions of personal greatness. As their master, he exemplified before them the way of the servant, even stooping to wash their feet.

2.4 Look not every man on his own things, but every man also on the things of others.

2.4 A Christian should not be so preoccupied with his own advancement that he cannot stop to render aid to others. The story of the Good Samaritan reveals this principle. Jesus told about a traveler who had fallen among thieves on the road from Jerusalem to Jericho. While he lay wounded on the wayside, other busy individuals hurried by. Those who walked past the beleaguered, helpless victim were religious men performing religious duties. Our devotions must not be devoid of compassion for the desperate needs we encounter daily.

2.5 Let this mind be in you, which was also in Christ Jesus:

2.5 The highest expression of true humility is found in the condescension of Almighty God in Christ. His example is a perfect pattern for us to follow.

Every individual carries a worldview. Our way of thinking is a product of our experiences, our education, and even our genetic disposition. This unique blend of influences is often referred to as a paradigm. Our personal paradigm is the lens through which we filter all new information. For each child of God, the primary influence on our mentality should be Christ.

It is imperative to study the life of Christ and adopt the mindset of Christ. The mind of Christ can only be fully grasped by absorbing his teachings. The Christian should become familiar with both the words he spoke and the behavior he modeled.

2.6 Who, being in the form of God, thought it not robbery to be equal with God:

2.6 The form of God. This term is not a reference to shape or outline. Rather, it is about the expression of the very essence of God himself.

Paul wrote to the Colosse believers that Christ was

actually "the image of the invisible God" (Colossians 1:15). The author of Hebrews calls him "the express image of his person" (Hebrews 1:3). Paul also recorded in II Corinthians 4:6 that a glimpse of the very "glory of God" can only be seen "in the face of Jesus Christ."

"God was manifest in the flesh" says Paul in I Timothy 3:16. "To wit, that God was in Christ, reconciling the world unto himself," he also records in II Corinthians 5:19. Jesus Christ is God himself expressed as a man among men.

It should be remembered that Paul was a Jewish scholar. Over and over his letters emphasize his authentic Jewishness. He leaves no doubt that he willingly identifies with fellow Jews. He wrote to Corinth, "Are they Hebrews? So am I. Are they Israelites? So am I. Are they the seed of Abraham? So am I" (II Corinthians 11:22).

He also insisted that his Jewish education qualified him for explaining Christ. He addressed this reality in Galatians 1:14, "And profited in the Jews' religion above many my equals in mine own nation, being more exceedingly zealous of the traditions of my fathers." He then further emphasized his role in expounding the revelation of Christ in light of Old Testament scripture. "But when it pleased God, who separated me from my mother's womb, and called me by his grace, to reveal his Son in me, that I might preach him among the heathen" (Galatians 1:15-16a).

He offers his pedigree in Philippians 3:5, confidently referring to himself as "an Hebrew of the Hebrews;

as touching the law, a Pharisee." The apostle never abandoned his Jewish identity.

It must be understood, therefore, that the Hebrew faith, at its core, was emphatically and unapologetically monotheistic. Take away its declaration that there is only one God and the entire religion falls apart.

With these facts in mind, it should be pointed out that not once in his writings, did Paul indicate a triune perspective of the Godhead. He clearly spells out the role of the Sonship of Christ regarding its necessity for our redemption and sanctification. He also informs the congregations of early Christendom about the vital work of the Spirit within the church. However, it is interesting to note that he addresses neither the son of God nor the Holy Spirit as separate, distinct persons from God the Father. At the same time, he retains the uniquely Jewish emphasis on the oneness of God. He refers at times to the Shema, the supreme monotheistic statement of Deuteronomy 6:4, "Hear, O Israel: The Lord our God is one Lord."

Thought it not robbery to be equal with God. Christ had every right to assert his deity. He would have been within his rights to demand recognition of his role as master of all and creator of earth – nevertheless he chose the more humble route.

2.7 But made himself of no reputation, and took upon him the form of a servant, and was made in the likeness of men:

2.7 **But made himself of no reputation**. Jesus didn't insist that he receive glory similar to the mighty rulers of the world. Instead, his birth took place in the obscurity of a stable. His childhood was largely uneventful in the small village of Nazareth. He was raised under the occupational tutelage of a lowly carpenter.

Jesus Christ didn't feel compelled to proclaim his own royalty. When he was accused of being a glutton and winebibber, he did not declare his kingship. When slandered for taking a meal with publicans and sinners, he did not feel pressured to even explain his actions. When interrogated by Pontius Pilate as to whether he considered himself to be a king, he said little.

At one point, the masses were so overwhelmed by his incredible miracles; they purposed to force him to consent to become their king (John 6:15). He quietly slipped away.

Took upon him the form of a servant. Though he was indeed God, Christ willingly took the lowliest of positions, that of a slave. It was a role that demanded complete obedience and subservience.

He taught his disciples, "If I then, your Lord and Master, have washed your feet; ye also ought to wash one another's feet" (John 13:14). His example of servitude was impeccable.

Nowhere was his total submission more evident than in the garden of Gethsemane. As a man, he prayed, "Not my will, but thine, be done" (Luke 22:42).

And was made. Passages dealing with our Lord's

sonship indicate a particular instance of incarnation. Terminology such as "pre-existing son" or "eternal son" should be avoided altogether. When broaching the subject, men who were clearly inspired by God used such terms as "begotten," "born," and "made."

John 3:16 calls Jesus the "only begotten son." The word "begotten" speaks of a specific beginning, not eternal pre-existence. Paul said, "But when the fulness of the time was come, God sent forth his Son, made of a woman, made under the law" (Galatians 4:4). These passages plainly indicate that something came to be that had not existed before. And that something was in the person of the son of God.

It should be acknowledged that Jesus indeed mentioned his previous glory. His prayer was this, "And now, O Father, glorify thou me with thine own self with the glory which I had with thee before the world was" (John 17:5). This does not refer to an ancient throne occupied by God the son. Revelation 5:12 specifies that the glory received at the throne of God is given to the "slain Lamb." Moreover, we are informed that this Lamb was "slain from the foundation of the world" (Revelation 13:8). Such symbology can only reference the salvific blueprint of God before the creation of mankind and in anticipation of man's subsequent fall into sin.

While Scripture tells us that the Son had glory before the world existed, we also learn that the crucifixion of Christ (the slaying of the Lamb) took place long before the birth in Bethlehem. The "majesty" (Hebrews 8:1) of the original high priest existed long before Moses was given the "pattern" (Hebrews 8:5) for the tabernacle in the wilderness and the commissioning of the high priests who served there.

The likeness of men. John wrote about him this way, "In the beginning was the Word, and the Word was with God, and the Word was God. The same was in the beginning with God. All things were made by him; and without him was not any thing made that was made" (John 1:1-3). Furthermore, he said, "And the Word was made flesh, and dwelt among us" (John 1:14).

As flesh and blood, he suffered temptation and ultimately triumphed (Hebrews 4:15). He accepted the penalty for disobedience without complaint. Paul described it: "For he hath made him to be sin for us, who knew no sin; that we might be made the righteousness of God in him" (II Corinthians 5:21). He was human enough to feel the both excruciating pain and humiliating shame that accompanied Calvary. According to Hebrews 12:2, he "endured the cross, despising the shame."

2.8 And being found in fashion as a man, he humbled himself, and became obedient unto death, even the death of the cross.

2.8 **And being found in fashion as a man**. Jesus Christ was observed to be fully human. He felt hunger and thirst. He experienced weariness. In his own hometown, he was not recognized for his greatness. The inhabitants of Nazareth pointed out the fact that they knew his family members.

As a man, he was awakened from sleep during a storm.

He spoke to the tempestuous wind and commanded it to be still. The disciples marveled at the immediate response. It had only taken a moment for the sea to calm. They questioned each other, "What manner of man is this, that even the wind and the sea obey him?" (Mark 4:41).

Perhaps a scripture referencing the God of Israel came to mind. Yahweh was the God "which stilleth the noise of the seas, the noise of their waves" (Psalm 65:7). And right before their eyes, here was a man able to do what had only been accredited to God.

He humbled himself. He was willing to undergo the humiliation of impoverishment. Paul wrote to Corinth that, amazingly, the Jesus they called Lord, "though he was rich, yet for your sakes he became poor, that ye through his poverty might be rich" (II Corinthians 8:9). He who had everything relinquished every possession and entitlement.

Jesus Christ also embraced the humiliation of becoming a student in the classroom of sorrow. He accepted his afflictions as a learning experience. Hebrews 5:8 says, "Though he were a Son, yet learned he obedience by the things which he suffered."

Finally, his cruel execution at Calvary signifies the ultimate humiliation. Christ made it clear that he gave his life voluntarily. He said, "No man taketh it from me, but I lay it down of myself. I have power to lay it down, and I have power to take it again" (John 10:18). He also told his followers, "Greater love hath no man than this, that a man lay down his life for his friends" (John 15:13).

2.9 Wherefore God also hath highly exalted him, and given him a name which is above every name:

2.9 Following the greatest expression of sacrifice, came the highest exaltation. One Greek scholar calls it a "super-eminent" exaltation.

Paul is not announcing the restoration of Christ to his previous throne. He is not hinting here that Jesus has received again the position of authority he held prior to the incarnation. The hyper-exaltation alluded to by the apostle is given as a direct result of Christ's unreserved subjection to the "death of the cross."

The supremacy of the name of Jesus is accentuated throughout both the gospels and the epistles. Emphasis upon this name is the climactic culmination of this hymn sung by the first century church, the stanzas of which are offered in Philippians 2:6-11. Becoming "highly exalted" is almost certainly connected to the "name which is above every name." This wonderfully special name is, in fact, a saving name. In Acts 4:12, we read, "Neither is there salvation in any other: for there is none other name under heaven given among men, whereby we must be saved."

John records the words of Jesus in prayer to the Father, when he said, "I have manifested thy name" (John 17:3). Christ also promised his disciples, "If ye shall ask any thing in my name, I will do it" (John 14:14). He also links the receiving of the Spirit to this all-powerful name. He pointed to the day of the Spirit-outpouring by saying, "But the Comforter, which is the Holy Ghost, whom the Father will send in my name, he shall teach you all things" (John 14:26).

2.10 That at the name of Jesus every knee should bow, of things in heaven, and things in earth, and things under the earth;

2.10 Paul, well-versed in Jewish law and prophecy, draws here from the writings of Isaiah. The apostle is fully aware that the passage from which he is quoting is adamantly monotheistic. Phrases, which appear in Isaiah 45, such as "there is no God else beside me" and "I am God and there is none else," are clear declarations of foundational Jewish oneness theology. Among these stands a statement by Yahweh himself regarding his own preeminence.

It is expressed this way, "I have sworn by myself, the word is gone out of my mouth in righteousness, and shall not return, that unto me every knee shall bow, every tongue shall swear" (Isaiah 45:23). Paul reaches back to this ancient text and squarely places the name of Jesus at the center of it. The eventual worldwide recognition of one powerful name is at the very heart of the fulfillment of Isaiah's long-ago prediction.

Every angel in heaven will bow before the Lord Jesus Christ. Every living creature on earth will eventually recognize his rightful claim to Lordship. Every fallen being of the nethermost regions will ultimately prostrate themselves before the superlative name of Christ.

2.11-30 And that every tongue should confess that Jesus Christ is Lord, to the glory of God the Father. 12 Wherefore, my beloved, as ye have always obeyed, not as in my presence only, but now much more in my absence, work out your own salvation with fear and trembling. 13 For it is God which worketh in you

both to will and to do of his good pleasure. 14 Do all things without murmurings and disputings: 15 That ye may be blameless and harmless, the sons of God, without rebuke, in the midst of a crooked and perverse nation, among whom ye shine as lights in the world; 16 Holding forth the word of life; that I may rejoice in the day of Christ, that I have not run in vain, neither laboured in vain. 17 Yea, and if I be offered upon the sacrifice and service of your faith, I joy, and rejoice with you all. 18 For the same cause also do ye joy, and rejoice with me. 19 But I trust in the Lord Jesus to send Timotheus shortly unto you, that I also may be of good comfort, when I know your state. 20 For I have no man likeminded, who will naturally care for your state. 21 For all seek their own, not the things which are Jesus Christ's. 22 But ye know the proof of him, that, as a son with the father, he hath served with me in the gospel. 23 Him therefore I hope to send presently, so soon as I shall see how it will go with me. 24 But I trust in the Lord that I also myself shall come shortly. 25 Yet I supposed it necessary to send to you Epaphroditus, my brother, and companion in labour, and fellowsoldier, but your messenger, and he that ministered to my wants. 26 For he longed after you all, and was full of heaviness, because that ye had heard that he had been sick. 27 For indeed he was sick nigh unto death: but God had mercy on him; and not on him only, but on me also, lest I should have sorrow upon sorrow. 28 I sent him therefore the more carefully, that, when ye see him again, ye may rejoice, and that I may be the less sorrowful. 29 Receive him therefore in the Lord with all gladness; and hold such in reputation: 30 Because for the work of Christ he was nigh unto death, not regarding his life, to supply your lack of service toward me.

2.11-30 Each individual voice will sooner or later publicly honor Jesus Christ as master of all. Paul shares with us the exact confession that will someday be uttered. Humanity as one will agree that "Jesus Christ is Lord."

The author knows full well what he is stating here. Very often throughout his writings, Paul has quoted from the Septuagint, the Greek translation of the Old Testament. Over 6000 times in the Greek Septuagint, the God of Israel is called kyrios, the Greek term for Lord. Yet, Paul is not reluctant to say that Jesus himself is, in fact, the kyrios, or Lord.

When Paul gives us echoes of Old Testament passages, he is never afraid to replace Jehovah or Yahweh with kyrios, which throughout the entire New Testament is used exclusively as a reference to Jesus Christ. For instance, Romans 10:13 is a quote from Joel 2:32, where the prophet says, "Whosoever shall call on the name of the Lord shall be delivered." Fully cognizant that the ancient text spoke of Yahweh, the God of Israel, Paul boldly concludes that Jesus is the fulfillment of the salvation plan of Yahweh because Jesus is, in essence, the very embodiment of the God of Israel. He sees no distinct separateness between the God of Abraham, Isaac, and Jacob of the Old Testament and the Savior introduced to us in the New Testament: the Lord Jesus Christ. The God of Israel and Jesus Christ are fundamentally viewed as one and the same.

Philippians 3

3.1 Finally, my brethren, rejoice in the Lord. To write the same things to you, to me indeed is not grievous, but for you it is safe.

3.1 The rejoicing of the Christian should not be about earthly possessions. Neither should you find joy in positions or titles. Instead, you should heed the advice of Paul when he wrote, "Set your affection on things above, not on things on the earth" (Colossians 3:2).

The practice of worship is a continual acknowledging of what the Lord has given and what the Lord has done. Setting aside time specifically for thanksgiving is a guaranteed way of renewing our joy. James directed our attention heavenward when he said, "Every good gift and every perfect gift is from above, and cometh down from the Father of lights, with whom is no variableness, neither shadow of turning" (James 1:17).

The Psalmist David sang, "My soul shall make her boast in the Lord: the humble shall hear thereof, and be glad" (Psalm 34:2). Throughout Scripture, the child of God is encouraged to find pleasure in the search for spiritual things. Christ insisted to his followers that "a man's life consisteth not in the abundance of the things which he possesseth" (Luke 12:15). Grasping for worldly glories leaves the soul empty and the inner man dissatisfied.

Human beings can seek for joy in sinful pursuits or they can seek for joy in the will of God, but it is not possible to find joy in both. One or the other must be relinquished. Jesus said, "No man can serve two masters: for either he will hate the one, and love the other; or else he will hold to the one, and despise the other. Ye cannot serve God and mammon" (Matthew 6:24).

Recognizing the severity of life's challenges should not diminish the believer's capacity for joy. Rather, correctly identifying and facing the joy thieves head on greatly enhances the Christian's enjoyment in life.

3.2 Beware of dogs, beware of evil workers, beware of the concision.

3.2 Paul cautions saints against unhealthy influences. "Dogs" here are not the lovable pets of today's world. They were mostly viewed as dirty scavengers, carrying diseases dangerous to the population. Had you lived in ancient times, you almost certainly wouldn't let them get close.

"Evil workers" refers to those who endeavor to coax others to join their perverse ways. Paul is warning against something more than mere sinners. He is telling the Philippian believers that they will encounter those with evil intentions, to ensnare them in false doctrine and perverse philosophy. Paul's plea to Corinth comes to mind, when he wrote, "But I fear, lest by any means, as the serpent beguiled Eve through his subtlety, so your minds should be corrupted from the simplicity that is in Christ" (II Corinthians 11:3).

"Concision" is not speaking of the covenant of circumcision carefully observed by Jews for multiplied generations. Instead, it actually refers to self-mutilation. No doubt, the line of reasoning behind this activity was, if removing excessive flesh in the Hebrew rite of circumcision was pleasing to God, then multiple cuts and gashes inflicted throughout the body must surely be that much more impressive.

The devotees of Baal behaved similarly. I Kings describes the scene, "And they cried aloud, and cut themselves after their manner with knives and lancets, till the blood gushed out upon them." These types of rituals were extreme and were foreign to the people of God.

3.3 For we are the circumcision, which worship God in the spirit, and rejoice in Christ Jesus, and have no confidence in the flesh.

3.3 The qualifications for true New Testament circumcision are listed. Paul has also discussed this subject in his letter to the church at Colossae. He informed them, "Ye are circumcised with the circumcision made without hands, in putting off the body of the sins of the flesh by the circumcision of Christ: Buried with him in baptism" (Colossians 2:11-12).

Those who are included in the new covenant "worship God in the spirit." The church is a spiritual entity. Paul echoes what Jesus said to the woman at the well. He told her, "God is a Spirit: and they that worship him must worship him in spirit and in truth" (John 4:24).

Ephesians 4:4 tells us, "There is one body, and one Spirit." In some scriptures, it is called "the Spirit of Christ" (Romans 8:9). In other instances, it is referred to as "the Spirit of the Lord" (II Corinthians 3:17). Additionally, it is referenced as "the Spirit of God (Romans 8:9) or simply, "the Spirit" (Romans 8:26). This is the same "Holy Ghost" that was poured out on the Day of Pentecost (Acts 2:1-4).

It is this spirit-infilling that is essential for Jesus Christ truly becoming one's master. It is also necessary if one is to arrive at the revelation that Jesus of Nazareth is the embodiment of the God of Israel. Paul asserted that "no man can say that Jesus is the Lord, but by the Holy Ghost" (I Corinthians 12:3).

Christians should intentionally refuse to trust in flesh. Humanity, at its greatest, is severely limited. Educators assume that if one knows better, then one will do better. This is not always the case with human beings. Paul also wrote, "For I know that in me (that is, in my flesh,) dwelleth no good thing: for to will is present with me; but how to perform that which is good I find not" (Romans 7:18).

3.4 Though I might also have confidence in the flesh. If any other man thinketh that he hath whereof he might trust in the flesh, I more:

3.4 If anyone had reasons for boasting of fleshly accomplishments, Paul did. If there were any individuals who could pride themselves in a highly disciplined lifestyle, it was Paul. However, he adamantly refused to allow such self-exaltation.

3.5 Circumcised the eighth day, of the stock of Israel, of the tribe of Benjamin, an Hebrew of the Hebrews; as touching the law, a Pharisee;

3.5 Paul offers an abbreviated pedigree indicating his authentic Jewishness. He is not flaunting his origins as a Hebrew blue-blood. Rather, he is modestly presenting a resume, which validates his expertise in Old Testament studies. Understanding his depth of knowledge about the law of Moses, we should pay attention when he uses the old covenant to teach us about Christ.

From the beginning of his life, he was immersed in Jewish culture. He can point specifically to the tribe of his origin. Benjamin was the tribe from which the first king of Israel was taken. The people of Benjamin were also praised for their bravery in battle. To be counted among the offspring of Benjamin was to be numbered with the highest tiers of Hebrew society.

In an age when it was more common for Jews to speak the Greek language, Paul was fluent in Hebrew. He was able to peruse the ancient texts in the original versions and explain them eloquently.

He was a member of the most devout order of Judaism, the Pharisees. These men endeavored to scrupulously follow the law. They meticulously examined each minute detail of Scripture.

While they were to be commended for their cautious obedience, Jesus rebuked them for their neglect. While they carefully paid tithes on the smallest pinch of spices, they were far less dedicated in their relationships with fellow human beings. He said, "Woe unto you, scribes and Pharisees, hypocrites! For ye pay tithe of mint and anise and cummin, and have omitted the weightier matters of the law, judgment, mercy, and faith: these ought ye to have done, and not to leave the other undone" (Matthew 23:23).

3.6 Concerning zeal, persecuting the church; touching the righteousness which is in the law, blameless.

3.6 Such was the devotion of Paul, that upon the rise of Christianity, he resorted to the most extreme behavior – aggressively campaigning for the slaughter of believers – intending to squelch the spread of the Christian faith.

Even a Pharisee, with his microscopic lens finely tuned to magnify the slightest discretion in others, would not have been able to discover a flaw in Paul's faithful observance of the law. In the midst of a religious fellowship holding the highest of standards, Paul stood high above the rest.

3.7 But what things were gain to me, those I counted loss for Christ.

3.7 There had been a day when Paul took great satisfaction in his rankings among the Jewish elite. And yet upon his conversion, he was more than willing to lose this coveted status.

In the past, every step was brilliantly strategized to propel him into ever loftier positions of fame and power. During his years among the Jewish leaders, his every footfall was only in a forward direction. However, in proclaiming the gospel of Christ, he incurred the wrath of those from whom, such a short time before, he had sought to gain approbation. In accounting terms, Paul transferred his standing among the elite from the "profit" column to the "loss" side of the ledger.

3.8 Yea doubtless, and I count all things but loss for the excellency of the knowledge of Christ Jesus my Lord: for whom I have suffered the loss of all things, and do count them but dung, that I may win Christ,

3.8 He willingly laid every personal advantage aside for the profound salvation experience he found in Christ. He eagerly risked his life in order to offer others the same opportunity.

There was absolutely no resemblance between the Saul of the past and the Paul of the present. Never would he choose to go back to the old days of prominence and authority. He never seemed to have looked back and wished for the time when he had clout with the high priest and other Jewish elders. In that era, he carried "letters to Damascus to the synagogues, that if he found any of this way, whether they were men or women, he might bring them bound unto Jerusalem" (Acts 9:2). The old Saul of Tarsus apparently had the power of life and death in his hand.

Instead of promoting his own advancement, Paul publishes the life and teachings of an executed criminal. The Pharisees who were still adhering to cardinal

Jewish doctrine, would count such an investment of energy and sacrifice as wasted.

The word "dung" refers to either human excrement or spoiled food unfit for consumption. In both cases, it belongs in the sewer. This is how vociferously Paul turns his back on his previous pursuits. His lifelong agenda for making a name for himself, in light of the cause of Christ, was worthless.

3.9 And be found in him, not having mine own righteousness, which is of the law, but that which is through the faith of Christ, the righteousness which is of God by faith:

3.9 The Pharisees widely broadcasted their "own righteous." Jesus made it clear that when they gave alms, it was "that they may have glory of men" (Matthew 6:3). He also upbraided their public practice of prayer, when he said, "For they love to pray standing in the synagogues and in the corners of the streets, that they may be seen of men" (Matthew 6:5). Furthermore, he cautioned his disciples against following their method of fasting, when he pointed out, "They disfigure their faces, that they may appear unto men to fast" (Matthew 6:16). Upon receiving a revelation that Jesus Christ was truly Lord Almighty, Paul abandoned this Pharisaical paradigm of spirituality.

Paul recognized he was beckoned to a higher level of righteousness. The "righteousness of the law" is fulfilled in those who have been baptized by "the Spirit" (Romans 8:4). The greatest reward for the outward observance of the commandments was to receive the "praise of men" (John 12:43). This is the shallow righteousness of religious tradition. The righteousness derived from faith in Christ is never fraudulent or pretentious.

Faith is not a passive component of Christian creed. Faith is actually revealed in the seeker. The writer of Hebrews announced, "But without faith it is impossible to please him: for he that cometh to God must believe that he is, and that he is a rewarder of them that diligently seek him" (Hebrews 11:6). In the beatitudes, Jesus taught, "Blessed are they which do hunger and thirst after righteousness: for they shall be filled" (Matthew 5:6). Rather than resting in an affirmation of eternal security, Paul was driven by a passionate desire for more of Christ and his righteousness.

3.10-11 That I may know him, and the power of his resurrection, and the fellowship of his sufferings, being made conformable unto his death; 11 If by any means I might attain unto the resurrection of the dead.

3.10-3.11 Paul displays an intense spiritual hunger. The word "know" represents intimacy. This closeness is initiated by joining Christ in his death, burial, and resurrection.

Resurrection is only possible by sharing in his death. Paul wrote, "Knowing this, that our old man is crucified with him, that the body of sin might be destroyed, that henceforth we should not serve sin" (Romans 6:6). He also testified, "I am crucified with Christ" (Galatians 2:20) and "I die daily" (I Corinthians 15:31). He practiced the inward work of repentance regularly.

Calvary was not some remote idea of substitutionary atonement. But it was a reality that played itself out in daily experience. Taking up one's cross through the act of repenting is a vital element of the overcoming life. In Romans 6:2, Paul asked rhetorically, "How shall we, that are dead to sin, live any longer therein?"

Our suffering brings us into a deeper connection with Christ. Paul doesn't express resentment toward the trials he endured. The pain simply inspired him to look forward. A snapshot of his outlook is caught perfectly when he said, "For I reckon that the sufferings of this present time are not worthy to be compared with the glory which shall be revealed in us" (Romans 8:18).

3.12 Not as though I had already attained, either were already perfect: but I follow after, if that I may apprehend that for which also I am apprehended of Christ Jesus.

3.12 With a long, impressive list of accomplishments to his credit, Paul never rested on his laurels. There were always new goals. Cities still waited to be reached with the Gospel. Churches yet unborn still tarried in the womb, eager to come alive and flourish for the sake of Christ. Ministers were yet to be trained in preaching the truth and making disciples.

3.13 Brethren, I count not myself to have apprehended: but this one thing I do, forgetting those things which are behind, and reaching forth unto those things which are before,

3.13 The apostle refused to dwell in the past. He possessed a laser beam focus. Yesterday's achievements were set aside and distractions were ignored. He resisted the temptation to languish in self-pity, although quite probably he was confined to a prison cell. He wasted no time railing against the injustice of his situation. He had spiritual objectives clearly in mind at which he aimed.

3.14 I press toward the mark for the prize of the high calling of God in Christ Jesus.

3.14 At the heart of his motivation, was his calling from God. It was no mere vocation or career. It was more than a pleasant way to spend his time. The call was a consistently powerful influence that never let up. It pulled him ever higher. It tugged at him always in an upward direction.

From the moment on the Damascus Road, when he was arrested by God, his world was never the same. That day, he looked up toward heaven and asked, "Who art thou, Lord?" (Acts 9:5). The answer he received to his inquiry made a lasting impression. He discovered that Jesus was truly the God of Abraham, Isaac, and Jacob. This was the beginning of a lifetime of service. Thereafter, he would dedicate himself to spreading the word that Jesus is Lord. Namely, it could be described this way: Paul, a Jew, would spend the remainder of his days proclaiming, far and wide, that the God of Israel had come to earth to save his people from their sins, through Christ the Messiah. This was a daunting task with numerous challenges – it certainly ranks as a "high calling."

3.15 Let us therefore, as many as be perfect, be thus minded: and if in any thing ye be otherwise minded, God shall reveal even this unto you.

3.15 Believers should feel persuaded in the same manner Paul did. A distinct mark of maturity is a lack of self-obsession and a wholehearted pursuit of the calling of God, whatever that may be. If one has not yet adopted this Christ-oriented mindset, by the Word and the Spirit, God will redirect the individual's thinking and show him how to be transformed into the "new creature" he has intended him to become all along.

3.16 Nevertheless, whereto we have already attained, let us walk by the same rule, let us mind the same thing.

3.16 All believers are urged toward unity in the body. While diversity is acknowledged and celebrated among saints, all should unify around a common purpose. This requires effort on the part of church members. Paul exhorted the growing congregation in Ephesus for the purpose of togetherness, by putting it this way, "Endeavouring to keep the unity of the Spirit in the bond of peace" (Ephesians 4:3). A well-developed church is an assembly fastened tightly together by the "bond of peace." An earnest desire for missional oneness should pervade both the Christian's actions and attitudes.

3.17 Brethren, be followers together of me, and mark them which walk so as ye have us for an ensample.

3.17 Paul unashamedly required a disposition toward submission in those who recognized his apostleship. Ministerial authority was taught and expected as a matter of principle. Throughout his epistles, Paul emphasized the necessary role of church government. Church officials were held to a high code of conduct. Believers were instructed to "esteem them very highly in love for their work's sake" (I Thessalonians 5:13). Those who respected and obeyed the teachings of Paul were approved examples before the flock. Others were urged to walk in their footsteps.

3.18-19 (For many walk, of whom I have told you often, and now tell you even weeping, that they are the enemies of the cross of Christ: 19 Whose end is destruction, whose God is their belly, and whose glory is in their shame, who mind earthly things.)

3.18-3.19 An element of rebellion had become manifested in the Philippian body and Paul warns that a significant number have been swayed. A specific opposition to certain Bible doctrines had become obvious before a wide array of church members. Evidently, the early church had its share of backsliders and rebels. The object of contention was the refusal to embrace a personal cross.

Paul is a man of such a tender heart that the tears flow freely as he addresses this difficult subject. He is broken over the negative effects these recent developments have produced within the congregation at Philippi. He is also quite emotional over the undesirable destination at which these belligerent individuals will eventually arrive. Just as the self-will of Satan invited his fall from heaven, likewise these individuals will be destroyed.

These nefarious activities spring up from a deep well of unwholesome appetites. So misguided are these dark personalities, that sins which should cause a person to blush in shame are instead committed and published proudly as if they are noble attainments.

These individuals seek no godly, spiritual guidance. They only live for the moment. They scoff at those who hold an eternal perspective. Such persons maintain a slavish devotion to their depravity. They hold an almost worshipful reverence for their own base tendencies. The priority of the true Christian is foreign to them. Paul spoke of it when he wrote, "While we look not at the things which are seen, but at the things which are not seen: for the things which are seen are temporal; but the things which are not seen are eternal" (II Corinthians 4:18).

Apostle John warned against this earthly clasping of trifling playthings when he said, "Love not the world, neither the things that are in the world. If any man love the world, the love of the Father is not in him. For all that is in the world, the lust of the flesh, and the lust of the eyes, and the pride of life, is not of the Father, but is of the world. And the world passeth away, and the lust thereof: but he that doeth the will of God abideth forever" (I John 2:15-17).

3.20 For our conversation is in heaven; from whence also we look for the Saviour, the Lord Jesus Christ:

3.20 In contrast to the behavior of apostates, the redeemed navigate by a different compass. The people of God have embraced a heavenly lifestyle, in anticipation of the return of the Lord Jesus Christ. Paul has taught that "the day of the Lord so cometh as a thief in the night" (I Thessalonians 5:2). Moreover, his writing insists to believers, "Therefore let us not sleep, as do others; but let us watch and be sober" (I Thessalonians 4:6).

3.21 Who shall change our vile body, that it may be fashioned like unto his glorious body, according to the working whereby he is able even to subdue all things unto himself.

3.21 The second coming of Christ will bring about the most profound transformation yet. John described this transformative event with these words, "Beloved, now are we the sons of God, and it doth not yet appear what we shall be: but we know that, when he shall appear, we shall be like him; for we shall see him as he is" (I John 3:2). We, who have waited faithfully for Christ, will undergo a complete metamorphosis into the likeness of Christ.

Paul detailed elsewhere how quickly this radical transfiguration will take place. He said, "In a moment, in the twinkling of an eye, at the last trump: for the trumpet shall sound, and the dead shall be raised incorruptible, and we shall be changed" (I Corinthians 15:52).

Paul further explained this future notable occasion by saying, "For the Lord himself shall descend from heaven with a shout, with the voice of the archangel, and with the trump of God: and the dead in Christ shall rise first: Then we which are alive and remain shall be caught up together with them in the clouds, to meet the Lord in the air: and so shall we ever be with the Lord" (I Thessalonians 4:16-17). For the Christian, setting his sights on the coming of the Lord will realign his priorities with the "high calling of God in Christ Jesus" (Philippians 3:14) instead of the "weak and beggarly elements" (Galatians 4:9) of this world.

The power that eventually changes the "vile body" into a reflection of Jesus Christ is the same force that ultimately will triumph over every principality and ruler in existence on earth. The culmination of the work of Christ is the moment he will "put down all rule and all authority and power" (I Corinthians 15:24).

Philippians 4

4.1 Therefore, my brethren dearly beloved and longed for, my joy and crown, so stand fast in the Lord, my dearly beloved.

4.1 The success of the saints at Philippi was proudly borne as a trophy of victory. Of all the accolades Paul has received, the faithfulness of his spiritual offspring ranks as the chiefest joy. His anticipation of delivering a glorious bride to the heavenly bridegroom is apparent in his second letter to Corinth. He declared, "For I am jealous over you with godly jealousy: for I have espoused you to one husband, that I may present you as a chaste virgin to Christ" (II Corinthians 11:2).

4.2 I beseech Euodias, and beseech Syntyche, that they be of the same mind in the Lord.

4.2 Paul pinpoints an apparent dispute between two prominent members possibly causing church-wide division. He addresses them by name and urges them toward reconciliation. The name Euodias means "prosperous journey" while the name Syntyche means "pleasant acquaintance." By beseeching them, Paul is using the strongest language to exhort them to live up to their names.

4.3 And I intreat thee also, true yokefellow, help those women which laboured with me in the gospel, with Clement also, and with other my fellowlabourers, whose names are in the book of life.

4.3 Paul continues addressing the theme of unity. The word "intreat" suggests that he has the authority to demand the laying aside of differences and both parties coming together for a common cause. His usage of the term "true yoke-fellow" implies there is yet much work to be done. He also bestows honorable mention on certain saints who had toiled tirelessly for the sake of the gospel achieving a high and noble reputation in Philippi.

What a notable privilege, to be mentioned by name in an epistle penned by the outstanding missionary Paul. However, Paul mentions a category of even greater significance. The most blessed honor of all is to have one's name written in the "book of life."

A book of names is referenced in Exodus 32:32-33, where it reads, "Yet now, if thou wilt forgive their sin—; and if not, blot me, I pray thee, out of thy book which thou hast written. And the Lord said unto Moses, Whosoever hath sinned against me, him will I blot out of my book."

The book of Revelation refers to the book of life a number of times. Apparently, it contains a record of those who have eternal life. Revelation 20:15 states, "And whosoever was not found written in the book of life was cast into the lake of fire."

4.4 Rejoice in the Lord always: and again I say, Rejoice.

4.4 Though the author has touched upon some sensitive issues, he reiterates the necessity of rejoicing. Despite the unpleasant situations within the congregation, he insists that the continual practice of focusing on the positive will yield spiritual benefits. Paul is committed to repeating the vital truths that make for a healthy environment.

4.5 Let your moderation be known unto all men. The Lord is at hand.

4.5 Extremism should be avoided when possible. A balanced approach should be the goal in all areas of Christian living. Moderation is defined as "not being unduly rigorous, being satisfied with less than one's due, sweet reasonableness, forbearance."

Believers should always keep in mind the soon return of the Lord. A reminder such as this should temper our worldly passions and alter our impulses toward carnality.

4.6 Be careful for nothing; but in every thing by prayer and supplication with thanksgiving let your requests be made known unto God.

4.6 Do not be overwhelmed by worry. Those who bring their own petitions and the needs of others consistently before God in prayer, along with an attitude of gratefulness for gifts already received, have the antidote for being overcome by excessive anxiety.

4.7 And the peace of God, which passeth all understanding, shall keep your hearts and minds through Christ Jesus.

4.7 "And" connects the effect of verse seven with the cause in the preceding verse six. The prayer life of the believer is what taps into the incredible peace that comes from God.

This level of peace can't quite be adequately described. The Psalmist spoke of this peace when he said, "Great peace have they which love thy law: and nothing shall offend them" (Psalm 119:165). Isaiah 26:3 says, "Thou wilt keep him in perfect peace, whose mind is stayed on thee: because he trusteth in thee."

"Shall keep" is a military term, indicating that God's peace is standing guard, diligently maintaining watch, at all times, over the heart and mind of the Christian.

4.8 Finally, brethren, whatsoever things are true, whatsoever things are honest, whatsoever things are just, whatsoever things are pure, whatsoever things are lovely, whatsoever things are of good report; if there be any virtue, and if there be any praise, think on these things.

4.8 We are given guidelines for the proper care and feeding of the godly mind. One should be intentional about the seeds that are planted within one's thoughts. One should ever be vigilant about the influence of friends and acquaintances. One should always be mindful of the content that is consumed, whether from media, social networking, or other venues. That which does not measure up to this clearly detailed criteria, should be shunned or discarded.

4.9 Those things, which ye have both learned, and received, and heard, and seen in me, do: and the God of peace shall be with you.

4.9 A great resource for wholesome thinking and Christ like action is found in what has been taught in the church by word and by example. Moreover, a worthy place for discovering material appropriate for investing in the mind is in the word of God. It is not enough for the Christian to simply have "learned" or "received" or "heard" or "seen" – he must "do" what he has been instructed, in other words, he must get into the habit of putting his Christianity into practice. Thus engaged, he will witness the presence of peace.

4.10 But I rejoiced in the Lord greatly, that now at the last your care of me hath flourished again; wherein ye were also careful, but ye lacked opportunity.

4.10 After a period of time during which he received little from them, the Philippian church members resumed their care for Paul. This was cause for deep gratitude. The apostle does not hold their season of silence against them.

4.11 Not that I speak in respect of want: for I have learned, in whatsoever state I am, therewith to be content.

4.11 He refused to become desperate for outward signs of their compassion. Instead, he used the opportunity as a learning experience. Paul arrived at a highly refined sense of contentment. External conditions did not create internal crises. His soul remained at an even keel, despite the surrounding troubled waters.

4.12 I know both how to be abased, and I know how to abound: every where and in all things I am instructed both to be full and to be hungry, both to abound and to suffer need.

4.12 Paul resisted the temptation to allow the praises of men to swell him up with pride. Conversely, he adamantly refused the despair that often accompanies painful afflictions and disappointing setbacks. Through the influence of the Spirit, his emotions were kept in check. Whether he was criticized or applauded, he never responded in an extreme manner. Highly disciplined in mind and spirit, he avoided both intense highs and despondent lows, the pitfalls of leadership since the dawn of creation.

4.13 I can do all things through Christ which strengtheneth me.

4.13 The seasoned apostle definitely understands who enables him in trying moments. His usage of "Christ" here is particularly telling. He gives us the Greek word for Messiah, or "anointed one." Certainly, if anyone understands the power of the anointing, Paul does. He discussed this subject extensively in his letters. In I Corinthians 2:4, he says, "And my speech and my preaching was not with enticing words of man's wisdom, but in demonstration of the Spirit and of power." He was fully aware that the ancient prophets taught that "the yoke shall be destroyed because of the anointing" (Isaiah 10:27).

Perhaps he is indicating more than simply the empowerment of the Spirit. Elsewhere, Paul has insisted that the Christian life is impossible without the "Spirit of Christ" (Romans 8:9). But we should also observe that Scripture urges us to draw strength from Christ's example. The author of Hebrews pointed to him as the perfect illustration of endurance, when he wrote, "For consider him that endured such contradiction of sinners against himself, lest ye be wearied and faint in your minds" (Hebrews 12:3).

Paul also has exalted Christ as the superlative expression of pure love. He instructed the church at Ephesus, "Husbands, love your wives, even as Christ also loved the church, and gave himself for it" (Ephesians 5:25). The most beautiful and authentic declaration of true affection is in sacrificial love. And nowhere else was it more emphatically proven than in Christ willfully laying down his life.

Not only are we empowered by the indwelling of the Spirit; we are also inspired by the incomparable demonstration of love for mankind that Christ Jesus displayed at Calvary.

4.14-16 Notwithstanding ye have well done, that ye did communicate with my affliction. 15 Now ye Philippians know also, that in the beginning of the gospel, when I departed from Macedonia, no church communicated with me as concerning giving and receiving, but ye only. 16 For even in Thessalonica ye sent once and again unto my necessity.

4.14-4.16 The Philippian congregation retained a special place in the heart of Paul. At times, Philippi was the only church body to give significantly and sacrificially to his ministry. This group of believers were not merely followers, they were leaders, especially in the categories that mattered. When it came to contributing money, among other things, they were selfless and magnanimous. These Christians didn't take their behavioral cues from other churches. They willingly stood alone in supporting their founding missionary.

4.17 Not because I desire a gift: but I desire fruit that may abound to your account.

4.17 Paul didn't give his life to ministry for the purpose of monetary advantage. The large hearted giving by the Philippian congregation was simply proof of the increase of their fruitfulness. Paul himself lived by the stringent qualifications he stipulated to others as necessary for a preacher of the Gospel. He spelled them out to the fledgling pastor Titus, by saying, "For a bishop must be blameless, as the steward of God; not self-willed, not soon angry, not given to wine, no striker, not given to filthy lucre" (Titus 1:7). Paul practiced what he demanded of others.

4.18 But I have all, and abound: I am full, having received of Epaphroditus the things which were sent from you, an odour of a sweet smell, a sacrifice acceptable, wellpleasing to God.

4.18 The apostle rejoiced in the offering he received from Philippi. He also took great joy in the safe arrival of the messenger Epaphroditus. He used an Old Testament analogy for the manner in which their gift was accepted. When a burnt offering met the exact specifications given by Jehovah God, he called it a pleasant aroma – a sweet savour. Obviously, God relished the sacrifice ritual. The moment that Israel approached his presence and asked for his favor and forgiveness by placing an unblemished beast on the altar, to be slaughtered as an act of worship; this gesture of voluntarily giving one's best was very special to God. Paul indicates to the saints at Philippi that their sacrifice has been just as noteworthy.

4.19 But my God shall supply all your need according to his riches in glory by Christ Jesus.

4.19 Every individual Christian has needs that only God can meet. Every church body has needs that only God can meet. Paul reminds the believers in Philippi that the reservoir from which they are supplied is inexhaustible. David had written, "The earth is the Lord's, and the fulness thereof; the world, and they that dwell therein" (Psalm 24:1). If everything on earth belongs to God, how much more should we trust him to provide for us from his heavenly storehouse?

4.20-23 Now unto God and our Father be glory for ever and ever. Amen. 21 Salute every saint in Christ Jesus. The brethren which are with me greet you. 22 All the saints salute you, chiefly they that are of Caesar's household. 23 The grace of our Lord Jesus Christ be with you all. Amen.

4.20-4.23 Customary salutations are in order before closing. Paul sends greetings to every church member in Philippi. No one is excluded. Perhaps most importantly, he includes salutations from the saints living under the very nose of Cesar himself. There were devout Christians who worked daily in the palace at Rome. This is a striking testimony about the power of the gospel. In an era of intense persecution against Christians, the powerful new-birth message had infiltrated the most formidable fortress of all, the household of Cesar. While the Roman rulers worked feverishly, attempting to squelch the spread of the Christian message, the gospel of Christ was so transformative and far-reaching, that it penetrated the very inner circle of government authority, ultimately bringing about the triumph of the kingdom of Christ over the kingdom of Cesar.

www.ingramcontent.com/pod-product-compliance
Lightning Source LLC
Chambersburg PA
CBHW040418100526
44588CB00022B/2862